THIS BOOK BELONGS TO :

Made in United States
Troutdale, OR
11/26/2023

14956793R00058